Good Housekeeping

TRADITIONAL HOUSEHOLD HINTS & TIPS

To Ellie

Acknowledgements
With thanks to Gill Smedley, formerly of the Good Housekeeping Institute

Good Housekeeping
TRADITIONAL HOUSEHOLD HINTS & TIPS

LINDA GRAY

This edition published in 1994 by Limited Editions

1 3 5 7 9 10 8 6 4 2

Text copyright © Linda Gray 1994

Linda Gray has asserted her right to be identified as the author of this work.

All rights reserved. No part of this publication may be reproduced, stored in a retrieval system, or transmitted in any form or by any means, electronic, mechanical, photocopying, recording or otherwise, without the prior permission of the copyright owners.

The expression GOOD HOUSEKEEPING as used in the title of this book is the trade mark of the National Magazine Company Limited and the Hearst Corporation, registered in the United Kingdom and USA, and other principal countries of the world, and is the absolute property of the National Magazine Company Limited and the Hearst Corporation. The use of this trade mark other than with the express permission of The National Magazine Company Limited or the Hearst Corporation is strictly prohibited.

First published in the United Kingdom in 1994 by
Ebury Press, Random House, 20 Vauxhall Bridge Road, London SW1V 2SA

Random House Australia (Pty) Limited
20 Alfred Street, Milsons Point, Sydney, New South Wales 2061, Australia

Random House New Zealand Limited
18 Poland Road, Glenfield,
Auckland 10, New Zealand

Random House South Africa (Pty) Limited
PO Box 337, Bergvlei, South Africa

Random House UK Limited Reg. No. 954009

A CIP catalogue record for this book is available from the British Library.

Editor: Jane Middleton *Design*: Jerry Goldie

Typeset by Puretech Corporation, Pondicherry, India
Printed in China

Contents

Introduction
6

How to Clean Everything
8

Extra Care for Special Items
37

Pest Prevention
47

Make Do and Mend
52

Good Plain Cooking
58

Caring for Clothes
66

Traditional Decorating Tips
76

Gracious Living
83

Safety First
93

Index
94

Introduction

A HOME kept clean and comfortable with the minimum of effort and expense has been the dream of women throughout the ages. 'Household management will be a feature of *Good Housekeeping*,' promised the magazine in 1922, declaring that 'the time spent on housework can be enormously reduced without any loss to comfort'.

All true – though of course many readers of the time employed a maid, and sometimes a cook and a nanny, to lighten the domestic load. Manuals from the early part of this century are full of budgets, timetables, and advice on how to run the home with live-in staff, a daily maid, or (horrors) only a woman to do the laundry. But as the years went by, magazines tacitly acknowledged that readers were increasingly managing on their own, and by the war years their pages were crammed with economical hints and tips for making light of housework.

Though few women now start the day by laying a fire or blackleading the grate, much of the advice is just as

Introduction

relevant today as it was in the past. This book contains a selection of the most useful hints, passed on by readers and culled from the archives – including those of *Good Housekeeping*, whose early copies are filled with traditional tips on homecare. Many use everyday storecupboard materials that are cheaper than proprietary brands and just as efficient; others are common-sense tips that make you wonder, 'Why didn't I think of that?' Try them – and see how both your surroundings and your budget can benefit.

How to Clean Everything

__B__ack in the eighteenth century John Wesley declared that cleanliness was next to godliness — advice that must have been taken to heart, judging from the number of traditional tips on the subject. Certainly, in the past, women fought a constant battle against soot from open fires and mud walked in from unmade roads, though it's likely that the soft light shed by gas or oil lamps hid a considerable layer of grime — hence the need for a thorough spring-clean when the sunshine threatened to reveal all. Here are some of their most useful household hints.

The Essential Home-Cleaning Kit

THESE STORECUPBOARD buys should meet most of your cleaning needs. Test on a hidden area to check for damage and, for safety, wear rubber gloves when applying them, don't smoke, and keep a window open. *Never* mix cleaning agents unless instructed, and be sure to store them out of reach of young children. If you splash any on your skin, rinse immediately with plenty of cold water. Throw away any rags that have been used with flammable products such as turpentine.

Ammonia can be diluted with water to keep glass, ceramic tiles and even jewellery sparkling and free from grease. Use a cup of ammonia in a bowl of detergent solution to remove a build-up of water-based polish from hard floors. Dab a little dilute ammonia on to grease stains on clothes – test an inconspicuous patch first and repeat with plain water.

How to Clean Everything

Bicarbonate of soda neutralizes acid stains and counteracts smells. For general cleaning, dissolve a heaped teaspoonful in $1/2$ pint (275 ml) of warm water – excellent for fridges, larders and work surfaces, For stains, use neat on a damp cloth or apply mixed with a little water to make a paste.

Bleach (sodium hypochlorite) kills germs, removes stains, and destroys mould and mildew. Use neat for lavatories or paths, or diluted for soaking white cottons and linens.

Borax softens water and breaks down grease. Use it on enamelled sinks and baths, glass and tiles. Pour a hot solution down sinks and drains to prevent blockages.

Lemon contains citric acid, wonderful for restoring tarnished metal or removing lime scale. Use neat or in water, depending on the extent of the problem, or dip a piece of lemon in salt for a mildly abrasive action.

Linseed oil feeds and protects natural wood. Old-fashioned hardware stores should stock it.

Methylated spirit is an alcohol that should be used with care, because it is flammable. Use it to shift sticky marks and stubborn labels, glue residues and ink from felt tips.

How to Clean Everything

Salt can be used for cleaning as well as cooking. Scouring with salt removes stains on dishes and chopping boards, and it can be used with lemon (see above), to increase its effectiveness.

Soda crystals (washing soda) are splendid for clearing sink wastes and drains and soaking soiled laundry, but they're very strong. Avoid contact with aluminium, because soda can pit the surface.

Turpentine is a useful solvent. You're more likely to find white spirit (sometimes called turpentine substitute) in use today.

Vinegar is one of the most versatile home remedies. It is ideal for removing greasy marks from tiles, windows, furniture and floors. For general cleaning, add one teaspoonful of white vinegar to $^1/_2$ pint (275 ml) of tepid water; for stubborn dirt, use half water, half vinegar.

KITCHEN

INGREDIENTS THAT are kept conveniently in the larder, such as lemon juice, bicarbonate of soda, vinegar and salt, can play an important part in keeping the kitchen fresh and clean. These are the kind of remedies that would have been employed in the 1860s, when Mrs Beeton wrote that a dirty kitchen was 'a disgrace to both mistress and maid'.

To spring-clean floor tiles

TRY THIS classic remedy for removing an unsightly build-up of water-based polish and making sure floor tiles are sparkling. Make sure the water is not too hot, and open the windows to disperse fumes.

Make up a bucket of detergent solution using warm water. Add 1 teacup of ammonia to the solution and mop thoroughly. You'll need to wear rubber gloves and use a scrubbing brush to remove the tidemark at the edge of the floor and stubborn stains, which can be shifted with wire wool. Rinse with clean water and mop dry.

To keep drains clear

MAKE A point of flushing the waste pipes clean once a week, using the following method.

Pour ½ teacup of soda crystals into the sink waste and run the hot tap for a minute. If the outlet is clogged, use freshly boiled water to shift the grease.

For clean larder shelves

LARDERS AND food cupboards should be kept clean to prevent mould and pests. Here's an easy way to make sure they're immaculate.

Line each shelf with 4 to 6 layers of wallpaper or lining paper, cut to size. (Don't use pasted varieties, which contain chemicals.) Remove one layer each week or so, before restocking with groceries, so the surface is always clean.

Scouring saucepans

THIS WAS a necessary chore in the days before nonstick finishes. In grand houses, it was usually delegated to the scullery-maid, whose hands would become raw from working with soda and salt; thank heavens for rubber gloves! Steel, aluminium and cast-iron saucepans often need more than a quick wash to remove burnt-on food.

Here are some traditional treatments to try.

Fill the pan with water and add a sliced onion and 1 dessertspoon of salt. Boil then leave to soak overnight; the residue should wash away easily.

Add hot water to the pan with 2 teaspoons of cream of tartar. Simmer for 20 minutes, then leave to cool. Rinse and wipe clean.

Rub a little baking powder into the pan and leave overnight. The pan should come clean when washed the next morning.

Rinse saucepans that have been used for milk or potatoes immediately after use, to prevent staining.

Quarry tiles

QUARRY TILES have made a deserved comeback. Good to look at, they're easy to care for, virtually indestructible and designed to resist damp. Here's the traditional way to look after unglazed tiles.

Make up a bucket of hot detergent solution, adding 4 oz (125 g) of washing soda. Apply this to the floor with a stiff broom. Rinse well and mop dry. Finish by applying a small amount of non-slip liquid wax polish and buffing with a cloth tied over a mop to bring out the shine.

To remove lime scale from kettles

VINEGAR IS a traditional kitchen standby for dealing with lime scale.

Cover the kettle element with equal parts of vinegar and water and bring to the boil. Switch off and leave overnight. Rinse thoroughly. Fill with water, boil and empty again before using.

How to Clean Everything

To clean a vacuum flask

VACUUM FLASKS often become tainted after they have been used for a while or have been filled with soup or strong tea. Here's how to clean them.

Put 1 tablespoon of bicarbonate of soda into the flask and fill with boiling water. Leave the flask overnight and rinse out well before using.

❖

To clean cloudy glasses

IF YOUR tumblers don't seem to sparkle as they used to, try this simple remedy for brightening them up.

Fill the glasses with water and add 1 teaspoon of ammonia to each one. Leave overnight then wash thoroughly and rinse in hot water.

Quick Tips

Vinegar diluted in warm water can be used to freshen the bread bin.

Bicarbonate of soda on a damp cloth cleans kitchen work tops.

A hot, strong solution of *soda crystals* removes grease from extractor fans.

Cold water was traditionally used to soak (and strengthen) new brooms.

Lemon peel in washing-up water acts as a rinse aid.

A *marble* in the kettle helps to prevent furring.

Methylated spirits will clean cork table mats.

BATHROOM

LIME SCALE and hard water marks soon make bathroom fittings look shabby. Dripping taps are often the culprit, so have them fixed before you tackle the stain.

To remove lime scale

TRY THE following remedies to deal with lime scale. They are acidic and abrasive, so apply carefully and use for the minimum time necessary on ceramicware and enamelled baths only.

Apply neat lemon juice to the stain, working in with an old toothbrush, or rub very gently with a lemon dipped in salt then rinse thoroughly. Alternatively, mix a little borax to a paste with white vinegar and apply to the stain, then clean as usual.

Stained baths and basins

THESE CAN be cleaned with a variety of spirits and oils. Use on ceramic and enamelled baths only, because solvents can damage plastic baths.

Equal quantities of turpentine and linseed oil applied on a soft cloth will remove most discolouration and stains. Clean off with hot soapy water and rinse thoroughly after use. If the bath is very badly stained, try neat paraffin on stubborn spots.

❖

Three ways to treat wall tiles

DECORATIVE TILES were so popular on fireplaces, washstands and splashbacks that it's no wonder there are a number of useful tips for keeping them bright.

To brighten discoloured tiles, try rubbing the surface with a paste made from silver sand (available from builders' merchants) and paraffin. Rinse clean and buff to a shine.

Polish tiles with milk and water to add shine to the glaze.

Clean hard water film by wiping the tiles with neat dilute vinegar on a soft cloth. Leave for 10 minutes then rinse off.

❖

Quick Tips

Apply *bleach* on an old toothbrush to clean grouting between tiles, then rinse off.

A length of *spiral wire*, pushed down the plug hole, will remove hair and scum.

Rub *liquid detergent* on mirrors to prevent them steaming up.

Soak natural sponges in *vinegar and water* (1 tablespoon to 1 pint/550 ml) to prevent sliminess.

LIVING ROOM

TRADITIONAL MATERIALS that wear well and go on looking good are favourites for the living room. Here are some tried and tested ways of caring for them.

Dry scrubbing

THIS USED to be a popular way of spring-cleaning upholstery, removing dirt with minimal dampness.

Dissolve $1/2$ cup of pure soap flakes or grated toilet soap in 2 pints (just over 1 litre) of hot water. Leave to stand until it forms a soap jelly, then take $1/2$ cup of the jelly and add to 1 pint (550 ml) of warm water in a bowl. Beat with an eggwhisk until it resembles shaving foam. Dip a nail brush into the suds only (not the water) and treat a small area of upholstery at a time, testing on an inconspicuous place. Remove the foam with a stockinette cloth wrung out in plain water, taking care not to wet the fabric. Finish by raising the pile with a soft brush.

Bran tub tips

HOUSEMAIDS AND housewives alike found bran invaluable for refreshing upholstery and loose covers. Its fats and mineral salts made it a good substitute for soap, its vegetable acids fixed colours, and the starch in it stiffened fibres. Try it in the final rinse for cotton covers and curtains, but keep it for deep shades and rich patterns only. If the fabric is pale or has a white background, add a teaspoon each of white vinegar and salt to the final rinse instead of using bran to make the colours glow.

Tie 4 oz (125 g) bran firmly in a muslin bag then place in a deep pan and pour over 4 pints ($2\frac{1}{4}$ litres) of boiling water. Leave for half an hour, then remove the bag and add the water to the final rinse.

For fixed upholstery, brush thoroughly to remove as much dust as possible. Put a generous handful of bran into a basin and rub it into the furniture with a clean cloth. Brush away both bran and dirt, and sponge with cool water any spots that remain, blotting frequently with a clean towel.

Glass decanters

GLASS DECANTERS can become stained and musty if they are stored with wine left in and the stopper in place.

To remove a jammed stopper, brush round the neck of the decanter and the stopper decanter with warmed cooking oil. Leave in a warm place overnight, then tap gently all round with a wooden spoon. With luck, the stopper should slide out.

You can then clean the decanter by filling it with warm soapy water and adding either 1 cup of white vinegar and 1 tablespoon of salt or the same amount of crushed eggshell. Leave to soak for several hours, shaking occasionally, then rinse and leave upside down to dry.

To cherish a piano

'DUST IT, wash it, USE it,' implored *Practical Housekeeping* magazine in 1938. Then, as now, owners were advised to stand the instrument against an inside wall and to avoid sharp changes in temperature and humidity in order to preserve its tone. Here are some comprehensive tips for cleaning.

After dusting the piano case, wring out a lint-free rag in hand-hot water, fold into a pad and sprinkle with a few drops of polish made from 1 part boiled linseed oil to 2 parts turpentine. Polish with long, smooth strokes, following the grain of the wood and treating a small section at a time. Follow immediately by rubbing vigorously with a clean, dry cloth to remove ingrained dirt.

To clean the ivories, sprinkle colourless spirit (such as gin or vodka) or methylated spirits on to a dry rag or wipe with a damp rag. Ebony keys should simply be buffed with a duster.

To look after paintings

PROTECT PAINTINGS from damp and help them hang straight at the same time. This method is particularly useful for paintings hung from picture rails.

Cut a cork in half and glue the pieces just above the base of the picture frame at the back. Hang the painting and shave away layers of cork if necessary until it hangs straight. The cork will prevent the picture frame from touching the wall and should ensure a good circulation of air behind it.

❖

Cabinet drawers

TO HELP cabinet drawers slide smoothly, treat in the following way.

Remove each drawer from its runners and polish the sides and back well. Rub the runners with soap or dressmaker's chalk, then replace. Unless the drawer is badly warped, it should open and close with ease.

Quick Tips

Use *warm water and washing soda* solution to clean wicker and cane.

Apply water with a *plant spray* to keep wicker supple.

Dissolve a teaspoon of *sugar in the juice of a lemon* and apply to hearth tiles and surround to keep them bright.

A *hot steam iron*, held above chair and sofa arms for a few seconds, will revive flattened upholstery.

Replace washed *loose covers* while still damp, so they stretch to fit.

Try *turpentine* to remove ring marks on wood, rubbing along the grain.

Spray *silicone polish* on curtain rails to make the drapes pull smoothly.

BEDROOM

To air musty cupboards and drawers

FURNITURE OFTEN acquires an old, stale smell when it is unused for a while. Before you air it, it's worth checking to see if there are any pinholes in the wood and small heaps of dust – the signs of woodworm. This needs treating chemically so that the worm doesn't spread throughout the house.

Crumple sufficient newspaper to fill the cupboards or drawers loosely. Leave slightly open for several days so the paper and ink can absorb damp and odours, then remove. Finish by placing the furniture outside to air, if possible. Add pieces of dried lemon peel or a drop of vanilla essence to keep the drawers smelling sweet.

Lace curtains

LACE CURTAINS add a pretty, traditional touch to bedrooms and are fast replacing nets. To make sure both look their best:

Hang panels while still wet after laundering, to prevent shrinking.

For a crisp finish, add 1 tablespoon of sugar to the last rinse of the wash.

Dye discoloured lace in cold tea to turn it a traditional creamy-beige.

❖

To clean a mattress

TRY THIS tip from the 1930s, which works wonderfully on stains.

Moisten 1 tablespoon of powder starch with sufficient liquid detergent (washing-up liquid will do) to make a paste. Apply to the stain and leave to dry, then brush off with a stiff brush. Any remaining marks can be removed with a damp cloth sprinkled with a few drops of ammonia or 10% hydrogen peroxide.

Quick Tips

A teaspoonful of borax and a tablespoonful of washing soda in warm water will keep hairbrushes clean and fresh.

Add *half a cup of borax and a teaspoonful of ammonia* to water, then soak washable pillows in it to make them sweet and clean.

Use *methylated spirits* for cleaning minors.

How to Clean Everything

ROUND THE HOUSE

To clean windows

SPARKLING WINDOWS are traditionally taken as a sign of good housewifery, and there are a number of tried and tested methods for making them shine. Choose a cool, dry, but overcast day for window cleaning to minimize streaking, and don't try to treat the whole house at once – window cleaning is surprisingly tiring.

Make up a vinegar solution, using 2 tablespoons of white vinegar to a small bucket of warm water. Wring out a chamois leather in the solution and rub it systematically over the windows. Allow to dry, then buff to a shine with crumpled newspaper – the printing ink works wonders. Should it soil the window frames, finish by cleaning them with detergent solution.

To make an old-fashioned polishing cloth

THIS CLOTH picks up dust and polishes at the same time.

Put 1 tablespoon of paraffin and 1 tablespoon of vinegar in a basin then drop a clean duster in it. Let the duster absorb the liquid, then store it in a screw-top jar so it doesn't dry out.

Grease spots on carpets

GREASE SPOTS not only look unsightly but act as a magnet to dirt if they're not removed properly. What's needed is a solvent – but, according to an early copy of *Good Housekeeping*, using petrol can leave white marks on the carpet and so make the original problem worse. Try using turpentine instead: it shouldn't affect the colour, but test on a hidden part of the carpet first, just in case.

Dampen a piece of cloth with turpentine and rub over the spots until you're satisfied they have gone. Finish by rubbing gently with a dry white cloth to remove all traces of turpentine.

To clean paintwork

MAKE PAINTWORK shine with these traditional
spring-cleaning tips to revive it.

Take 2 buckets and fill one with cold water plus 1 teaspoon of ammonia, the other with handhot water plus 1 teaspoon of ammonia and some mild detergent (washing-up liquid will do) or soap powder. Use a lint-free cloth to wash the paintwork with the warm water solution, taking care not to rub. Rinse before it dries with the bucket of cold water, applying with a well-wrung chamois leather.

Remove stubborn marks by rubbing with a slice of lemon before washing with detergent solution.

To make the paintwork sparkle, add 1 tablespoon of turpentine, 1 dessertspoon of milk and 1 dessertspoon of liquid soap to 2 pints (just over 1 litre) of hot water. Apply with a soft cotton cloth.

Quick Tips

Petroleum jelly will loosen stiff latches and bolts.

Weak *vinegar solution* removes the film of grease and dirt from carpets.

Stale bread will remove marks from wallpaper.

Salt will shift soot from carpets – brush both up together.

Shoe polish or soft crayon will disguise scratches on furniture. Apply along the grain with a soft cloth.

Silver sand, brushed over wooden floors, removes grease.

Brush *iodine* into deep gouges to disguise damage to wood.

Lay *raw potato slices* over mud marks on carpets to help remove them.

Sweep before dusting when cleaning hard floors – the broom will raise the dust.

Stain Removal

Speed is the best stain-removing method of all. Blotting a stain with a clean, absorbent cloth (a towel will do) can remove all trace of disasters – even red wine and coffee. Left it too late? Then try these methods, recommended in the early part of the century. Note that they are for washable fabrics only.

Blood – soak in cold salt water.

Candlewax – scrape off as much as possible, then sandwich with blotting paper and press with a warm iron. Remove any colour from the candle by dabbing with alcohol – choose a colourless spirit.

Chocolate – sprinkle with borax and soak in cold water before laundering.

Coffee – rub fresh stains with glycerine then rinse with warm water.

Egg – soak in cold water before washing.

Engine oil – place a pad of fabric underneath to absorb the pigment, then loosen the grease with lard or olive oil, working towards the centre of the stain. Launder as usual.

Fruit juice – soak in milk for an hour before washing.

Grass – dab with methylated spirit or a paste made from equal parts of cream of tartar and salt, plus water.

Grease – apply a thick layer of powdered starch or talcum powder to the fabric and leave overnight. Brush off to remove both powder and stain. Alternatively, try ironing the fabric between several layers of blotting paper.

Ink – try soaking in milk. For red ink, spread mustard over the stain and leave for half an hour before laundering.

Jam – soak in a borax solution of 1 tablespoon borax to 1 pint (550 ml) warm water for half an hour before washing.

Mildew – treat white cotton and linen with bleach solution or rub when damp with soap, followed by white chalk. Wash and rinse as usual then hang in the sun to dry.

Milk or cream – treat with cold water first to remove the protein, then sandwich with thick wads of blotting paper and press with an iron to shift the fat.

Rust – soak for several hours in the water from boiling rice, or cover with a paste of equal parts of salt and cream of tartar plus water, or salt and lemon juice. Rinse and hang to dry in the sun.

Tar – scrape off as much as possible, then treat with oil of eucalyptus, removing the tar with a clean white cloth.

Wine – rinse in warm water then soak or sponge in a borax solution of 1 tablespoon borax to 1 pint (550 ml) warm water before washing. For dried stains, sprinkle with borax and pour hot water over.

Extra Care for Special Items

***P**recious metals and valuable antiques should be left to the experts, but how should you keep brass door furniture, gilt picture frames and elderly furniture in good repair? Here's how to treat those traditional materials that need a little expert knowledge and extra care.*

Extra Care for Special Items

To renovate cane

CANE CHAIR seats need expert attention once they've begun to fray, but you can make sagging seats taut again in the following way.

Protect the chair and seat surround by wrapping in plastic. Add 1 tablespoon of bicarbonate of soda to a basin of warm water. Work a little of the solution into the cane with a soft brush and wipe over with a cloth until quite wet. Turn the chair over and treat the underside. The seat should shrink as the chair dries, but avoid direct heat.

❖

To revive faded fabric

FOLLOW THIS tip from prewar dry-cleaners. Try it first on a seam or inconspicuous area of cloth to test for damage.

Take an offcut of the fabric or a scrap of material that's similar in shade to the faded fabric and wet with carbon tetrachloride. Open the windows to disperse fumes. Rub into the discoloured fabric to remove grease and bring out the colour.

Extra Care for Special Items

To clean bamboo

WORK OUTSIDE, if possible, on a warm, dry day.

Add 1 tablespoon of borax and 1 cup of soap flakes to a bucket of warm water and scrub the bamboo with a clean shoebrush. Rinse thoroughly with salt water and allow to dry. Finish by polishing with a little linseed oil.

❖

Alabaster

LAMPS AND ORNAMENTS made of alabaster were very popular in the early part of this century. Here is some advice from Asprey's (who should know) for removing stains.

Start by sponging any stains with cotton wool dipped in a little white spirit. Alabaster is porous so simply buff with a clean dry cloth or use a well wrung-out chamois leather to remove surface soiling.

Extra Care for Special Items

A quick way to clean silver cutlery

THERE'S NO need to clean each piece individually if you're in a hurry – simply immerse it in this home-made solution.

Put 2 heaped tablespoons of washing soda and a handful of milk bottle tops in a washing-up bowl. Open the windows to disperse any fumes, then add the silver (make sure it touches the milk bottle tops) and top up with hot water until every item is covered. As soon as the mixture stops bubbling and the silver is clean, remove, rinse, and rub with a soft cloth. Put a little powder starch in the cutlery drawer to keep the silver bright.

❖

To clean gilt frames

KEEP MIRROR and picture frames sparkling with this traditional spring-cleaning treatment.

Dust the frame with a soft brush or a scrap of silk and then wipe gently with a small sponge dampened in equal parts of methylated spirits and water. Alternatively, use onion water to revive the colour. You can make this by boiling 4 onions in 1 pint (550 ml) of water (allow to cool before using). Dry with a chamois leather.

Extra Care for Special Items

To make leather glow

TRY FEEDING leather with this traditional egg, milk and water treatment.

Mix together the white of an egg and 1 cup of milk, then make up to 1 pint (550 ml) with cold water. Stir well and apply with a sponge. Allow to dry, then use a soft brush to make the leather shine.

❖

Polishing metal

MAKE METAL-POLISHING cloths to keep candlesticks, unlaquered door knobs and finger-plates burnished.

Mix together 4 parts of grated white toilet soap and 2 parts of jeweller's rouge with 20 parts of cold water. Soak offcuts of woollen cloth in the mixture, then remove and allow to dry, rubbing from time to time to keep the fabric soft. You will need about 1 oz (25 g) of the mixture to treat about 3 large cloths.

Extra Care for Special Items

Caring for brass

'A JOLLY door just doesn't have brass fittings if no one has time to polish them,' said one prewar household manual — and perhaps the decline in the use of solid brass has had as much to do with cleaning as with cost. Both brass and copper look beautiful when cared for and rather sad when not. If they're part of your home, try these useful tips.

If the piece is very tarnished, soak in a solution of vinegar and salt (about 1 tablespoon of salt to 1 pint/550 ml of vinegar) or washing soda. Wash in warm, soapy water, rinse and rub dry. Apply metal polish or clean with a lemon dipped in salt. Rub vigorously with a soft cloth to bring out the shine, then wash with warm water and ammonia solution (1 tablespoon of ammonia to 1 pint/550 ml water). Dry and buff as before.

Extra Care for Special Items

To restore mahogany

SEALED TIMBER or polished wood in good condition needs only conservative treatment, but if you have mahogany that's in poor repair, this approach will make it shine again.

If the wood is very dirty, wash with 1 tablespoon of vinegar in $^1/_2$ pint (275 ml) of water and rub dry. Wipe with turpentine or white spirit to remove grease and dirt then polish thoroughly with a clean, dry cloth. Soak another cloth in linseed oil and rub in well. Leave for 12 hours, then wipe off and buff to a shine using a soft, lint-free cloth. Three days later, repeat the linseed oil treatment. For a high gloss, finish by wiping down with warm water, dry well, and polish vigorously.

❖

To revive tortoiseshell

TORTOISESHELL LOSES its depth and shine with age. Here's how to restore its lustre.

Mix 1 teaspoon of jeweller's rouge with a few drops of olive oil to form a paste. Apply in circular movements, using a soft cloth, then buff to a shine.

Extra Care for Special Items

Make your own French polish

ALTHOUGH LARGE surfaces such as tabletops need expert attention, you can restore small items like mirror and picture frames yourself. To prevent an unsightly bloom appearing, make sure you work in an atmosphere that is free from damp and that the piece you are treating is warm and dry.

Make a polishing pad by covering a piece of lint or cotton wool with a soft cotton cloth and twisting it into an egg shape. Rub the item down with fine glasspaper, following the grain of the wood, and wipe clean. Make up the French polish by shaking together 1 pint (550 ml) of methylated spirits, 2 oz (50 g) of shellac, and the appropriate stain (both available from specialist decorators). Using a brush, apply a little of the polish to the pad then rub it lightly over the wood with a circular movement, applying more polish as required. Repeat three or four times, reversing the direction each time and using larger movements. Finish by sanding with very fine, worn glasspaper and give a final polish.

Extra Care for Special Items

Quick Tips

Rub gilt frames with *white spirit* to make them sparkle.

Use warmed *linseed oil* to add lustre to oak. Apply sparingly on a soft cloth along the grain and polish.

Save *potato water* after cooking – it removes tarnish from silver.

Olive oil brings a shine to brass.

A paste of *salt and salad oil*, left on for an hour, helps remove marks from polished wood. Remove carefully, then polish with a soft cloth.

Lemon juice and salt will clean cane.

Use *olive oil* to keep amber in peak condition.

Dip diamonds in *gin* to make them sparkle.

Wear pearls next to *your skin* as often as possible – its natural oils will make them glow.

Extra Care for Special Items

Remove stains on marble with *lemon*. Apply for a few minutes only, then rinse well.

A few drops of *methylated spirit* will clean onyx.

Equal parts of *linseed oil and white spirit* will bring a shine to slate hearths.

Warm beer helps to clean dark wood.

Equal parts of *methylated spirit and warm water* applied on a squeezed-out pad of cotton wool will remove discolouration on ivory piano keys.

Pest Prevention

Covering food, cleaning drains and disposing of rubbish in clean containers will deprive pests of nourishment and make them turn elsewhere for food. Despite this, plagues of pests can appear in the best-managed households, especially when the weather is hot. If you're afflicted and want to avoid potent chemicals, consider these traditional remedies.

Ants

BOILING WATER poured on the nest has the greatest effect, but if you can't find the nest, sprinkle the runs with cayenne pepper, cedar oil (from herbalists), fresh bracken, or a mixture of 1 part sugar to 2 parts borax.

Alternatively, you can make an ant trap.

To make an ant trap, spread the inside of a paper bag with marmalade and place it open where you see the ants appear. Leave overnight. Close the bag firmly next morning, when it should be full of ants, and burn.

❖

Bees and wasps

TRY NOT to destroy these insects – they are harmless unless provoked.

Try to restore bees to the garden. If they are buzzing against the window, place a glass against the pane and slide a sheet of paper between the glass rim and the window. Then you can carry the bee outside and release it.

If you are besieged by wasps, line your window sills with wasp-traps made from jars filled with a mixture of water, detergent and jam or honey. They will attract and drown the wasps.

Black beetles

EVERYONE HAS to cope with black beetles at some time. Here's how to do it.

Mix 4 parts plaster of Paris (from craft shops) with 1 part oatmeal and dust thickly over the floor. Alternatively, use equal parts of borax and white sugar near the skirting and cracks in the floor, where the beetles appear.

❖

Cockroaches

THIS IS also a useful way of preventing ants and silverfish.

Scatter borax or pyrethrum powder (made from chrysanthemums and available in hardware shops) over crevices, cracks in the floor and any trails you can see, to deter cockroaches.

Pest Prevention

Flies

HYGIENE IS the best way of preventing flies and stopping them from breeding. If you've no control over the source, hang bunches of basil and mint to repel them, or make your own fly papers, as follows.

Warm 8 fl oz (250 ml) of rapeseed oil and $3^{1}/_{2}$ oz (100 g) of resin, standing the container in a bowl of hot water. Spread thinly on to paper while still hot, cut into strips when cool, and hang them from the ceiling.

To prevent flies buzzing round the windows, polish the panes with a little liquid paraffin, buffing with a clean, dry cloth.

Mice

A GOOD way to deal with mice is to get a cat, but if you don't have one you can always try these traditional tips.

Plug mouse holes with a cork dipped in turpentine or cayenne pepper, or use balls of brown paper or newspaper dipped in eucalyptus oil. To protect food, scatter cayenne paper on larder shelves.

❖

Moths

MOTHS DISLIKE printer's ink, so wrap coats and heavy clothing in tissue paper followed by newspaper for storage. You can also use cedar oil to repel moths.

Pour a little cedar oil (available from herbalists) into a saucer or jar and leave in wardrobes and cupboards. (It will evaporate slowly and need replacing from time to time.)

Make Do and Mend

Waste was not a word the traditional housewife understood. Early copies of Good Housekeeping *and other homemaking magazines are filled with tips for squeezing that little bit extra out of clothes, food and furnishings, and you can see why when you examine the real-life budgets published at the time. The recent recession has made thrift a virtue once again, so here are some traditional tips that are well worth following.*

Sheets

WORN SHEETS needn't be thrown away. By cutting out the centre, which wears thin first, you can give them a new lease of life.

Cut the sheet in half lengthways, then turn 'sides to middle' by sewing the edges together and hemming the sides. Use a French seam for strength and smoothness.

Pure cotton or linen sheets are too valuable to be thrown away. Salvage what you can to make single sheets or mattress covers from double sheets, make pillowslips from worn singles, and cut up the rest for polishing cloths or glass cloths.

❖

To untie knots

TO UNTIE knots in laces or string, try this time-honoured process.

Place the knot on a level surface and strike gently with a wooden spoon several times, turning the knot over as you go. Insert the points of a small pair of scissors into the knot and gradually ease open. The knot should then unravel.

To repair broken ornaments

THIS WORKS best for items that do not require frequent washing – and definitely not in the dishwasher.

Mix a little plaster of Paris to a creamy paste with the slightly beaten white of an egg. Heat the pieces of broken china in an oven until they are as hot as you can bear, then apply the cement thinly to the broken edges. Press together and wipe away the surplus. Keep the pieces in place by propping or securing with a rubber band, and allow to dry. If the ornament is in several pieces, treat two at a time until the repair is complete.

❖

Firelighters

FIRELIGHTERS CAN be recycled from old newspaper, following this recipe.

Place several newspapers in a bucket or bowl, cover with water and leave until they're reduced to pulp. Wearing rubber gloves to protect your hands from newsprint, squeeze out the excess water and shape the paper into small, hard balls. Allow to dry out completely before using.

To patch wallpaper

PATCHING WALLPAPER can be surprisingly effective, so it's always worth keeping a spare roll.

Tear out a piece of wallpaper slightly larger than the damaged area but roughly the same shape. It's best to do this by hand so that the edges are irregular; shapes that are cut out always look obvious. Apply adhesive to the back and stick down well, taking care to match the pattern and using a roller to flatten the edges.

❖

Scorched linen

SCORCHED LINEN can be revived by following this time-honoured remedy – a mixture of Fuller's earth (available from chemists) and simple storecupboard ingredients.

Boil $^1/_2$ pint (275 ml) of vinegar with 2 oz (50 g) of Fuller's earth, 2 oz (50 g) of washing soda and a small, finely chopped onion. Stir well, strain and allow to cool. When cold, spread the paste over the scorch marks and leave to dry. Brush clean before laundering as usual.

Blinds

BLINDS WERE traditionally made from a stout green canvas known as holland, which was designed to protect furnishings from sunlight and fading. Roller blinds are the modern equivalent, and they can often be renovated in the same way. In some cases you'll be able to cut away any damage, which usually occurs at the bottom of the blind, without removing the fabric from the roller. If you want to disguise a larger area, try this method, which is suitable for plain fabrics and non-directional designs.

Unpin the blind from the roller and remove the bottom batten. Cut off the stained or damaged fabric at the bottom of the blind, then tack this edge to the roller and make a new slot at the other end for the batten.

Make Do and Mend

Quick Tips

Use *old stockings* (and tights) to pad wire coat hangers then cover with remnants of cloth.

Renovate place mats by covering them with *wallpaper coated in varnish*.

Remove scratches from a glass watch face by rubbing gently with *metal polish*.

Straighten bent sewing needles by dipping them in *hot water*, straightening them with your fingers, then tempering with cold water.

Open the bottom of brass or silver *polish tins* with a tin-opener when they appear empty – you will find that there is still some polish left.

Soften dried-up shoe polish with a little *turpentine*.

Place cotton wool in the *airing cupboard* for a few hours to make it increase in volume.

A tablespoonful of *bicarbonate of soda* in the wash softens water and saves on detergent.

Good Plain Cooking

'Plain cooking is, in fact, of more importance than any other,' said Eliza Acton in Modern Cooking for Private Families, *first published in 1845. Like Hannah Glasse, who wrote* The Art of Cookery Made Plain and Easy *a hundred years before, she concentrated on simple recipes – for 'common chicken pie', 'plain common fritters', 'cheap rice pudding' and 'buttered apples – excellent' – which provided cheap and nourishing family fare. And though the variety of food has increased enormously since then and sophisticated dishes can be bought ready-cooked, basic cooking skills never go out of fashion and neither will these simple tips, gleaned from centuries of good housewifery.*

To keep food fresh

IF THE fridge is full, try these ingenious ways of preserving food.

Stand celery in a jug of cold water, adding 1 teaspoon of sugar to each pint (550 ml).

Brush untreated lemons with egg or sour milk.

Revive limp lettuce by soaking it in cold water with a piece of coal.

❖

Poached eggs

HERE'S HOW to poach eggs the traditional way, without a special pan.

Place a metal pastry cutter in a pan of simmering water and break the egg into it. Add 1 teaspoon of vinegar to the water to keep the pan clean.

Baking powder

MIX YOUR own baking powder for economy, and keep it in a screw-top jar in a dry place.

Weigh out 2 oz (50 g) of bicarbonate of soda and 4 oz (125 g) of cream of tartar. Mix these together and then pass them through a sieve.

❖

Dried breadcrumbs

GOLDEN BREADCRUMBS for coating chicken and fish can be made economically from stale bread, following this wartime tip.

When using the oven, fill any spare shelves with stale slices and crusts of bread and leave until crisp and beginning to brown. Crush under greaseproof paper with a rolling pin. Allow to cool, then store in a screw-top jar or a tin.

Traditional ginger beer

THIS IS more than a thirst-quencher – it's a family entertainment too. Watch the 'ginger beer plant' grow as the brew ferments, and take care not to fill the bottles too full or they may explode and the ginger beer will end up on the ceiling.

Slice 2 lemons finely and put them into a clean bucket with ¾ lb (375 g) of sugar and 1 oz (25 g) of root ginger, slightly bruised. Pour over 8 pints (4½ litres) of boiling water and leave to cool. Just before the mixture is cold, add 1 heaped teaspoon of fresh yeast. Cover, leave for 24 hours, then remove any scum, siphon into bottles and cork tightly, securing the corks with string. Leave for 3 days then drink within a week.

❖

To glaze pies

FOR A rich brown crust on pastry, try this method as an alternative to brushing with egg.

Boil 2 tablespoons of milk with 1 tablespoon of brown sugar. When the sugar has dissolved, allow to cool then brush over the pastry. Bake as usual.

To refresh stale bread

STALE BREAD can be revived using this quick method.

Sprinkle the bread with water or milk, wrap it in kitchen foil and leave it in a hot oven for 5–10 minutes or until the crust feels crisp.

❖

Thrifty pudding

THIS RECIPE from the 1920s uses stale bread to make a delicious pudding.

Soak 1 lb (500 g) of stale sliced bread in water, then squeeze out the excess moisture and break up with a fork. Mix together with $^1/_2$ oz (15 g) cocoa, 3 oz (75 g) suet, 5 oz (125 g) sugar and 4 oz (100 g) sultanas. Stir in a beaten egg and pour into a well-greased mould. Steam for two hours and serve with custard.

To ripen fruit

IF YOU have a glut of part-ripened apples or tomatoes, finish what the sun has started by using a wire cake stand or grill tray.

Place the fruit on the wire tray in a well-lit place. There's no need to turn the fruit because good ventilation will make sure that it ripens evenly, without rotting or bruising.

❖

Cooking cauliflower

The smell of boiled cauliflower can be very unpleasant so to prevent the odour, simply add a bay leaf to the water in which you are boiling the cauliflower.

To whiten cauliflower, add half a cup of milk to the water in which it is being boiled. This helps prevent discolouration.

Quick Tips

Make up *mustard* with milk and a pinch of salt to keep it from drying out.

Make *oranges* easier to peel by standing them in freshly boiled water for five minutes first.

Rub *fish knives and forks* with lemon rind after washing to remove any taint.

If an *egg cracks* while boiling, add salt to the water to prevent the white escaping.

Put a *clean marble* in the pan when heating milk to save stirring.

Hang a linen bag filled with *powdered charcoal* in the larder to keep food fresh.

Good Plain Cooking

Roast *poultry* upside down until 30 minutes from the end of cooking, so the juices baste the breast.

Add 1 tablespoon of cold water to each egg white when making *meringues*, to double the quantity.

Out of eggs? Dissolve 1 tablespoon of *golden syrup* in $^1/_2$ pint (275 ml) of warm milk and use as required when making cakes.

Cut an *iced cake* with a knife dipped in boiling water to prevent cracking.

Add 1 teaspoon of *glycerine* to each 1 lb (500 g) of fruit when making jam, to improve the flavour.

Add dried *tangerine peel* to the pot for a fragrant cup of tea.

Caring for Clothes

Washing machines, easy-care fabrics and modern dry-cleaning techniques mean that looking after clothes is no longer the problem it used to be in the days when voluminous skirts, elaborate suits and starched collars were the rule. Nevertheless, running repairs and spot removal of stains are just as important today if clothes are to go on looking good, and if you like to invest in good-quality leather shoes it's certainly worth knowing how to care for them. You may find these tips come in handy.

Caring for Clothes

Darning

DARNING MAY have fallen from fashion, but it's a skill worth reviving, given the current cost of woollen sweaters. Darning mushrooms, which are designed to raise the area to be mended so it can be repaired easily, can still be found in haberdashery departments and draper's shops. Here are some other tips that may help.

When darning woollen (not synthetic) clothes, pre-shrink the darning wool in hot water before you use it to stop the darn contracting and puckering when the garment is washed.

Place a marble in the fingers when darning gloves to serve as a mini darning mushroom and make repairs easier.

Caring for Clothes

Perspiration odours

PERSISTENT PERSPIRATION odours can be removed from colour-fast clothes by treating them with simple storecupboard ingredients.

Soak the clothes for an hour in warm water and borax solution (use 2 teaspoons of borax to 1 pint/550 ml of water). Wash as usual and add a few drops of household ammonia to the final rinse. For the next few washes, add a spoonful of vinegar to the final rinse to remove any lingering odour.

❖

Suits

SHINY SUITS and skirts show sure signs of wear but they can be given another lease of life by restoring the texture. Here's what to do.

Rub the cloth lightly with a dry pumice stone and then brush well along the grain with a stiff clothes brush. Finish by pressing with a hot iron over a damp cotton cloth.

Zips

Z<small>IPS ARE</small> a nuisance to replace, but there are a number of tips to help you salvage an old one.

Zips often give way at the base, where they come under most strain. You can sometimes repair them by cutting away the broken teeth and repositioning the slider further up the zip. Sew up the base with stout thread, so the slider doesn't come away when the zip is opened.

Ease a stiff zip by opening it and rubbing the teeth on each side with a soft lead pencil. Always wash clothes with the zips closed to prevent further stiffness.

If a long zip is hard to reach when it's undone, attach a piece of stout cotton thread to the slider to help you close it.

To waterproof boots and shoes

SHOES ARE cheaper now than they were in the past, when the cost was a real worry to many families, and most soles are made from a durable (and non-slip) composite material that needs repairing less often. But it's still possible to buy boots or shoes with leather soles, which may benefit from this old-fashioned method of waterproofing.

Clean any mud and dirt off the shoes and dry the soles well. (If the shoes are new, scratch the soles with wire wool to give a better grip and prevent slipping.) Warm a little castor oil and apply with a small brush, working into the soles and making sure no oil splashes the uppers. After the oil has soaked in, give the soles two further applications and then leave the shoes in a warm place for 24 hours. Apply a further coat every 10 days to ensure that your feet are kept dry no matter how wet the weather.

Caring for Clothes

To make a laundry bag

ENCOURAGE YOUR family to pick up dirty clothes and prevent them getting trampled on by equipping everyone with a traditional laundry bag, which can be hung from a hook on the wardrobe or bedroom door. You'll need a remnant of cotton about 36 in (90 cm) wide, about a yard (1 metre) in length, plus a plastic or wooden coat hanger with a bar.

Fold the fabric in half lengthways and position the fold over the bar of the coat hanger. Hem the sides and the base, cutting away the front so that it is about 6 in (15 cm) shorter than the back. Now make a slit lengthways in the front for pushing the washing through and strengthen the edges with bias binding. Attach five large press studs just inside the back hem, so that it folds over and snaps shut at the front. When you collect the washing, simply open the fasteners and the washing will fall out into your laundry basket.

Caring for Clothes

Quick Tips

Dip a *clothes brush* in cold water to help pick up the dirt.

Clean coats and suits with a damp rag sprinkled with *ammonia*.

When cutting out fine fabrics, apply *nail varnish* to the cutting line to prevent fraying.

Shorten coat sleeves by making a *tuck in the lining*.

When removing buttons, insert a *comb* between the button and the cloth, so you don't accidentally snip the fabric.

To prevent *peg marks* when hanging out dresses and tops, thread a stocking through the sleeves and peg that to the line.

Rub suede with *glycerine* to remove grease.

Castor oil will soften stiff leather shoes.

Caring for Clothes

Add a tablespoon of *salt* to the rinsing water when washing silk to fix the colour and keep it soft.

A teaspoon of *Epsom salts* added to the final rinse keeps colours bright.

When handwashing sweaters, use a *colander* to remove excess water and stop them being pulled out of shape.

An *emery board* will remove shiny patches on suede shoes.

Glycerine gives a clear gloss to leather shoes.

Peg pleats individually when hanging out to dry – it saves ironing.

Turn knits and cotton jersey *inside out* before washing, to stop the fabric pilling.

Add a spoonful of *vinegar* to the final rinse to revive colours.

A little *dry soap or clear nail varnish* will stop runs in sheer stockings.

Caring for Clothes

Ironing

Do's and Don'ts

DO

Always iron motifs and embroidery on the wrong side.

Straighten fabrics with your palms, not fingers, to prevent undue stretching.

Stuff puffed sleeves with fabric or crumpled paper to make ironing easier.

Iron along the grain (warp threads).

Iron collars, cuffs and pockets wrong side first.

Iron fine fabrics through tissue paper.

Iron clothes over folded sheets to complete two jobs in one.

For a smart finish, rub yellow soap on the inside of a trouser crease before pressing the right side through a damp cloth.

Caring for Clothes

DON'T

Iron over buttons or piping cord – it makes the fabric shine and could cause holes.

Follow the hem when ironing a bias-cut skirt. Press towards the waistband instead to keep the skirt in shape.

Iron on the right side if the fabric is matt.

Iron crepe or chiffon while damp – wait until completely dry.

Iron velvet. Steam instead, by holding a hot steam iron a few inches above the fabric to raise the pile.

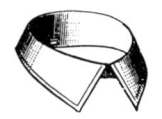

Traditional Decorating Tips

***D**ecorators of the past had to tussle with unforgiving materials like distemper, enamel, and flat oil paint, which shows every grease mark. As a result they developed a whole repertoire of short cuts and handy hints to cope with them. Although modern materials like solid emulsion, non-drip gloss and ready-pasted wallpaper have made decorating far easier, many home decorators today are amateurs rather than skilled craftsmen. Here are some traditional tips to help achieve a professional finish.*

Traditional Decorating Tips

To make paint go further

TRY THESE penny-pinching ways of getting the most out of a tin of paint.

Tie a piece of string over the top of the tin of paint to wipe away the excess after loading the brush with paint. This not only cuts down on waste but prevents runs.

Remove the lumps that can accumulate when liquid paint is stored, by straining it through an old pair of stockings or tights. Alternatively, secure an old stocking round the top of the paint tin with an elastic band and dip the brush into the paint, over the stocking, to prevent picking up grit or lumps.

Put a disc of waxed paper, film or foil over the paint to prevent a skin forming.

Pour small amounts of leftover paint into a screwtop jar and save for touching in and other repairs.

❖

Brushes

BRUSHES NEED looking after if they are to give smooth, professional results.

After cleaning, wrap the bristles in strips of cloth to prevent them drying out or curling. (The modern equivalent is plastic film.)

Drill a hole in the handle in order to hang the brush up after cleaning.

Restore neglected brushes by soaking them in hot vinegar, heated almost to boiling point.

Traditional Decorating Tips

To prevent paint smells

THE FOLLOWING remedies will also help prevent the headaches and sore throats that solvents can cause.

Place a saucer of milk in the room to absorb the odours.

Place half an onion high up – on a cupboard for example – to counteract paint smells. Alternatively, place half a peeled onion in a bucket of water in the centre of the room.

❖

Removing old paint

PAINTS OF the past may need removing before you redecorate, but you'll need to take special care.

Lead was used in gloss paint until comparatively recently, although most modern paints are now virtually lead-free. If you're renovating old furniture or paintwork in a period house, use liquid stripper rather than sanding to remove the paint and finish with wet and dry sandpaper, which can be moistened, to prevent lead dust in the air. Wear a mask and make sure there's adequate ventilation.

Glue size

THIS SEALANT makes a useful base for wallpaper, allowing you to slip the lengths into place. This recipe is especially for greasy walls, but try it for a flaking surface too.

Make up a size from standard wallpaper paste, following the instructions on the pack. Add 2 tablespoons of washing soda dissolved in $1/2$ cup of hot water and stir in well. Apply with a large brush and allow to dry. Finish by washing with a strong vinegar solution – 1 tablespoon to 1 pint (550 ml) of hot water.

❖

Rescuing wrinkled wallpaper

ALTHOUGH IT won't help where a whole length is affected, this emergency procedure is worth trying if there's an unsightly wrinkle in a prominent place.

Cut a cross in the blister with a razor blade and peel the paper back carefully. Apply a little paste and then press into place.

Traditional Decorating Tips

A decorative glaze

THIS GLAZE was originally designed as a non-slip polish for lino, but it can be used to give a clear, glossy finish to paintwork and wood. It's made from shellac, available from specialist decorating shops, which sell materials for paint treatments.

Mix 1 oz (25 g) of shellac with 1 cup of methylated spirits in a screw-top jar. Leave for 4 days, shaking every day. Thoroughly clean the surface to be varnished and apply with a soft paintbrush. Allow to dry, then repeat. Care for the glaze by wiping with a damp cloth.

❖

To clean your hands

WHITE SPIRIT tends to leave hands dry and cracked. You can avoid this by using cooking oil.

After a painting session rub your hands hard with about 1 teaspoon of cooking oil then wipe off well with a cloth.

Stripping wallpaper

THIS IS one task that is often more difficult nowadays than it used to be, given the popularity of strong adhesives and water-resistant finishes. Try the following methods of removing wallpaper.

Roughen the surface with a kitchen scourer.

Soak the paper with warm water applied with a sponge, or – carefully – use the steam from a boiling kettle.

Use a clean, sharp garden hoe to tackle areas that are out of reach.

❖

Removing screws

TO MAKE screws easy to remove, use these traditional tips.

Rub new screws across a bar of soap to prevent rusting.

Heat the screwdriver if you're finding it difficult to remove a screw.

Gracious Living

Who doesn't yearn for fresh flowers, potpourri and a table laid with starched linen? These finishing touches create a sense of occasion that can make all the difference to the atmosphere of your home. They needn't be time-consuming, because there are a host of simple traditional tips for making cut flowers last, using petals and spices to create potpourri or using scented oils to perfume cupboards and repel insects. Here are some short cuts to the domestic arts that help turn a house into a home.

Home-made potpourri

THIS FRAGRANT potpourri has a delicate, old-fashioned scent produced by the blend of petals and spices.

Collect sweet-scented rose petals and dry them on a sunny windowsill or in a greenhouse. Mix together equal quantities of lavender heads, vanilla pods, cloves and grated lemon peel, and crush finely with a pestle and mortar. Fill a jar or a bowl with alternate layers of dried rose petals and crushed spices. Stir or shake the potpourri regularly to revive the aroma.

❖

Pomanders

POMANDERS WERE favourites in Elizabethan times, when they were thought to protect against the plague.

Take a large orange and stud it with cloves until completely covered. Using a darning needle, insert strong thread from top to bottom, leaving enough at the top to form a loop. Knot at the base and hang in the wardrobe.

Scented tablets

MADE FROM wax and essential oils, these will perfume drawers and wardrobes and help keep moths at bay.

Melt 1 oz (25 g) of paraffin wax with 2 oz (50 g) of white petroleum jelly by putting them in a small basin then standing it in a bowl of hot water. Add 5 drops of oil of bergamot, 5 drops of essential oil of lavender and 2 drops of oil of cloves. Mix together well and allow to cool, then cut into squares and wrap in foil until needed.

❖

To make ironing easier

SWEETLY SMELLING clothes and easier ironing can be yours if you save fragments of soap. Save this tip for dry irons, as the soap may clog the vents in a steam iron's sole plate.

Cut the soap into slivers and place them on a sheet of white paper. Run a warm iron over them and then pass it over another sheet of paper to remove the excess soap. The iron should run smoothly and perfume the laundry at the same time.

Lavender bags

LAVENDER BAGS make the linen cupboard and clothes drawers fragrant and fresh.

Fill squares of cotton lawn with dried lavender heads and strips of dried lemon or orange peel, closing them by stitching or tying tightly with thread or narrow ribbon.

Stuff the toe of an old stocking with dried lavender and hang it from your wardrobe rail to scent your clothes.

Pad a wire coat hanger and fill with dried lavender and spices before covering with light cotton.

❖

To revive cut flowers

CUT FLOWERS will last much longer if kept in a cool place, but if yours have succumbed to the effect of central heating, give them a new lease of life as follows.

Plunge the base of the stems into boiling water and allow to cool. Cut a section from each stem and re-arrange the flowers in fresh cold water, adding a little charcoal or salt – especially good for roses.

Making flowers last

TO MAKE the most of the blooms — or if the flowers you buy look less than fresh — try the following tips to refresh and revive them.

First snip the ends off the flower stems, cutting away any white or discoloured areas, to help them absorb water. Add a tablespoon of sugar and a teaspoon of bleach to a bucket of lukewarm water and soak them in it for several hours so the stems fill with water.

Carnations should be cut just above the nodules on the stem so they will absorb more water.

Lilac has woody stems that need crushing to make the flowers last.

Lupins have hollow stems, as do dahlias and delphiniums. Hold the stems upside down and fill with water, then plug with cotton wool to prolong their life.

Poppy petals will take longer to drop if you burn the base of the stems before arranging.

Roses will last longer if you cut the stems at an angle and hold them in a pan of boiling water for a minute or two. (Cover the blooms with paper to protect them.)

Tulips have pliable stems that make wonderful arrangements but may bend too far. Wrap the tulips tightly in newspaper, which will soak up water, and stand them in a bucket of cool water overnight.

Violets can absorb water through their petals. Steep the bunch, flower-heads down, in cool water for an hour. This treatment will refresh gardenias too.

❖

To make a traditional posy

THAT VICTORIAN favourite, the posy, looks equally charming today. Although the stems are often wired so they stay in shape, a simple posy can be made from any flower that has pliable stems, such as violets or anemones.

Choose flowers with buds that are just beginning to open and soft stems – the longer the better. Take half a dozen in your left hand and add more blooms beneath these, holding them loosely and gradually twisting the stems as you go. When the flower heads form a dome shape, tie the bunch with raffia at the top of the stems and cut them to an even length. Insert a rose at the heart of the posy for a traditional touch.

❖

Pressing flowers

PRESSED FLOWERS look delightful, whether framed or used as bookmarks or decorative mats. The traditional way to press them was inside the family Bible, but for this purpose, a dictionary or telephone directory will do just as well.

Open the flower head carefully and arrange the petals and leaves gently in the centre of the book before closing it. (Make sure the pages are not coated or glossy; the paper should be porous to absorb moisture and oils.) To press leaves and sprigs of foliage, sandwich in newspaper and place beneath a rug or carpet until needed.

❖

How to dry fresh flowers

DRIED FLOWERS have a fragile beauty all of their own.
Here's how to capture it.

Plants that dry well include roses, hydrangea, honesty (remove the black seeds before drying), grasses, gypsophila, nigella, peonies, lavender and yarrow. Avoid sappy plants like daffodils and irises, which need specialist drying techniques. Pick flowers in the middle of a sunny day, when they will be at their driest, choosing those that are just about to open. Cut the stems to an even length and secure with an elastic band, which will stay tight as the stems shrink. Hang flowers with heavy heads upside down to dry from a rack or indoor clothes line, and stand grasses in a large dry container, separated into small groups by chicken wire. Keep all plants out of direct sunlight and damp, steamy areas, such as the kitchen. When the flowers are completely dry, wrap each bunch in tissue paper and store until needed in a wicker hamper, in a dry airy place. Arrange in a basket, using a ball of wet clay to support the stems.

Ways with fine wines

BOTH FINE and fortified wines need extra care if they're to be enjoyed to the full. Here's how to look after them.

If you have room, it's worth buying good wines young, when they are cheap, and laying them down to drink later. You don't need a cellar – a cool larder will do – but wines should be stored undisturbed, in the dark, at a temperature kept between (10–15° C) 50–60° F.

Lay fortified wines, such as sherry, madeira and port, horizontally until a few days before drinking. The bottle should then be kept upright, to allow the sediment to fall.

Too much bubbly? To keep champagne sparkling once you've opened it, put a spoon inside the bottle neck.

❖

Gracious Living

Quick Tips

To help *houseplants* flourish, water them three times a week with the water used to rinse out milk bottles.

A little *oil of citronella* (from herbalists) in a saucer will repel insects.

Smouldering *sprigs of lavender* placed in a saucer will freshen the atmosphere – but never leave them unattended.

Make sachets of *dried woodruff* (available from herbalists) and place them in the linen cupboard for that country-fresh scent.

Add a drop of *candlewax* to the centre of cut tulips to prevent them opening too quickly.

Tie sticks of *chalk* together with ribbon and hang in the wardrobe to absorb damp.

Add a few drops of *geranium and lavender* oils to water in a plant spray to freshen the air and counter infection too.

Safety First

MANY HOUSEHOLD cleaning products contain chemicals that can be harmful to your health, so it's important to store and use them safely.

DO

- store products well out of children's reach.

- work in a well-ventilated atmosphere – open doors and windows if you can.

- wear rubber gloves and protect your skin from splashes.

- dispose of rags used to apply flammable liquids (such as methylated spirits, turpentine or white spirit) with care. They can be combustible if kept in plastic sacks.

DON'T

- decant products into other bottles.

- mix products, unless instructed.

- smoke or work near an open fire or naked flame.

Index

alabaster, *39*
amber, *45*
ammonia, *9*
ants, *48*

baking powder, *60*
bamboo, *39*
bathrooms, *18–20*
baths, stained, *19*
bedrooms, *27–8*
beds, mattresses, *28*
bees, *48*
beetles, *49*
bicarbonate of soda, *10*, *17*
bleach, *10*, *20*
blinds, repairing, *56*
blood stains, *34*
boots, waterproofing, *70*
borax, *10*
bran, *22*
brass, *42*, *45*, *57*
bread: refreshing, *62*, *64*
  thrifty pudding, *62*
breadcrumbs, dried, *60*
brushes, *29*, *78*
buttons, removing, *72*

cakes, icing, *65*
candlewax, *34*
cane, *26*, *38*, *45*

carpets, *31*, *33*
cauliflower smells, *63*
china, repairing, *54*
chocolate stains, *34*
cleaning, *8–33*
clothes, *66–75*
clothes brushes, *72*
coat hangers, *57*
coats, *72*
cockroaches, *49*
coffee stains, *34*
cooking, *58–65*
cotton wool, *57*
cupboards, *27*
curtains, *26*, *28*
cutlery, silver, *40*

darning, *67*
decanters, *23*
decorating, *76–82*
diamonds, *45*
drains, *13*
drawers, *25*, *27*
dry scrubbing, *21*

egg stains, *35*
eggs, *59*, *64*, *65*

fabrics: cutting out, *72*
  reviving faded, *38*
firelighters, *54*

Index

fish knives, *64*
flies, *50*
floor tiles, *12, 15*
flowers: drying, *90*
   making them last, *87–8*
   posies, *88–9*
   pressing, *89*
   reviving cut, *86*
frames, gilt, *40, 45*
French polish, *44*
fruit, ripening, *63*
fruit juice stains, *35*

gilt frames, *40, 45*
ginger beer, *61*
glass, *16, 23, 30*
glaze, decorative, *81*
glazing pies, *61*
glue size, *80*
grass stains, *35*
grease stains, *31, 33, 35*

hairbrushes, *29*
hands, cleaning, *81*
houseplants, *92*

ink stains, *35–6*
insect repellant, *92*
ironing, *74–5, 85*

jam, *36, 65*

kettles, lime scale, *15, 17*
kitchens, *12–17*
knots, untying, *53*

lace curtains, *28*
larders, *13, 64*
laundry bags, *71*
lavender, *86, 92*
leather, *41, 72, 73*
lemon, *10, 17, 59*
lime scale, *15, 18*
linen, scorched, *55*
linen cupboards, *92*
linseed oil, *10*
living rooms, *21–6*
loose covers, *26*

mahogany, *43*
marble, *46*
mattresses, *28*
mending, *52–6*
metal, polishing, *41*
methylated spirit, *10, 17, 93*
mice, *51*
mildew, *36*
milk stains, *36*
mirrors, *20, 33*
moths, *51*
mustard, *64*

needles, straightening, *57*

oil stains, *35*
onyx, *46*
oranges, *64*

paint: brushes, *78*
   cleaning paintwork, *32*

Index

removing old, *79*
smells, *79*
to make paint go further, *77*
paintings, *25*
pearls, *46*
peg marks, *72*
perspiration odours, *68*
pest prevention, *47–51*
pianos, *24*
pies, glazing, *61*
pillows, *29*
place mats, *57*
pleats, drying, *73*
poached eggs, *59*
polish, French, *44*
polishing cloths, *31*
pomanders, *84*
posies, *88–9*
potpourri, *84*
poultry, roasting, *65*

repairs, *52–6*
ring marks, *26*
rust stains, *36*

safety, *93*
salt, *11*
saucepans, *14*
scented tablets, *85*
screws, removing, *82*
sheets, *53*
shoes, *57, 70, 72, 73*
silk, *73*
silver, *40, 45, 57*

size, *80*
slate, *46*
soda crystals, *11, 17*
sponges, *20*
stain removal, *34–6*
stockings, *73*
suede, *72, 73*
suits, *68, 72*
sweaters, *73*

tar stains, *36*
tea, tangerine peel in, *65*
tiles, *12, 15, 19–20, 26*
tortoiseshell, *43*
turpentine, *11, 93*

upholstery, *21–2, 26*

vacuum flasks, *16*
vinegar, *11, 17, 20*

wall tiles, *19–20*
wallpaper, *33, 55, 80, 82*
wasps, *48*
watch faces, *57*
waterproofing boots, *70*
white spirit, *81, 93*
wicker, *26*
windows, *30*
wine, *36, 91*
wood, damaged, *26, 33, 45*

zips, *69*